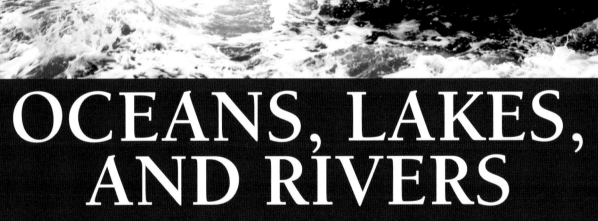

OCEANS, LAKES, AND RIVERS

Melanie Ostopowich

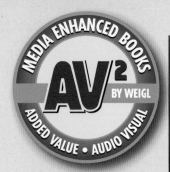

MEDIA ENHANCED BOOKS
AV² **BY WEIGL**
ADDED VALUE · AUDIO VISUAL

BOOK CODE

T 6 8 4 8 5 9

AV² by Weigl brings you media enhanced books that support active learning.

AV² provides enriched content that supplements and complements this book. Weigl's AV² books strive to create inspired learning and engage young minds for a total learning experience.

Go to **www.av2books.com**, and enter this book's unique code. You will have access to video, audio, web links, quizzes, a slide show, and activities.

Audio
Listen to sections of the book read aloud.

Video
Watch informative video clips.

Web Link
Find research sites and play interactive games.

Try This!
Complete activities and hands-on experiments.

Due to the dynamic nature of the Internet, some of the URLs and activities provided as part of AV² by Weigl may have changed or ceased to exist. AV² by Weigl accepts no responsibility for any such changes. All media enhanced books are regularly monitored to update addresses and sites in a timely manner. Contact AV² by Weigl at 1-866-649-3445 or av2books@weigl.com with any questions, comments, or feedback.

Published by AV² By Weigl
350 5th Avenue, 59th Floor
New York, NY 10118
Website: www.av2books.com   www.weigl.com

Library of Congress Cataloging-in-Publication Data

Ostopowich, Melanie.
  Oceans, lakes, and rivers / Melanie Ostopowich.
    p. cm. -- (Water science. Oceans, lakes, and rivers)
Includes index.
ISBN 978-1-61690-001-4 (hardcover : alk. paper) -- ISBN 978-1-61690-007-6 (softcover : alk. paper) -- ISBN 978-1-61690-013-7 (e-book)
1. Bodies of water--Juvenile literature. 2. Ocean--Juvenile literature. 3. Lakes--Juvenile literature. 4. Rivers--Juvenile literature. I. Title.
  GB662.3.O88 2011
  551.48--dc22
                              2009050980

Printed in the United States of America in North Mankato, Minnesota
1 2 3 4 5 6 7 8 9 0 14 13 12 11 10

052010
WEP264000

Project Coordinator Heather C. Hudak
Design Terry Paulhus

Photo Credits
Every reasonable effort has been made to trace ownership and to obtain permission to reprint copyright material. The publishers would be pleased to have any errors or omissions brought to their attention so that they may be corrected in subsequent printings.

Weigl acknowledges Getty Images as its primary image supplier for this title.

CONTENTS

When people drive cars or burn coal for power, a gas called carbon dioxide is released into the air. A great deal of this gas is absorbed into the ocean. Carbon dioxide reacts with sea water to create a kind of acid. Acid can dissolve the shells of animals such as clams, lobsters, and corals. This causes great damage to the oceans. To help solve this problem, people can drive less and use energy more wisely at home. Governments and companies can switch to sources of power that cause less **pollution**.

Studying Oceans, Lakes and Rivers

Earth has five oceans. They are the Indian, the Atlantic, the Arctic, the Pacific, and the Southern Oceans. Together, they cover more than 70 percent of Earth. About 97 percent of the world's water is located in oceans. Each ocean has smaller seas, bays, and gulfs. These oceans appear to be one large ocean.

For more than a century, scientists called oceanographers have studied the ocean. They have found millions of animal species and new **ecosystems**. Still, many ocean **habitats** remain unexplored.

Rivers and lakes can be found all over the world. Rivers are bodies of water that flow to lakes, oceans, and other rivers. Lakes are bodies of water surrounded by land. Rivers and lakes are home to many plants and animals that have adapted to life in and around water.

■ The deep sea anglerfish has adapted to life in the darkest parts of the Atlantic and Arctic Oceans. The female anglerfish has a piece of glowing flesh dangling above her mouth. This attracts other fish for the anglerfish to eat.

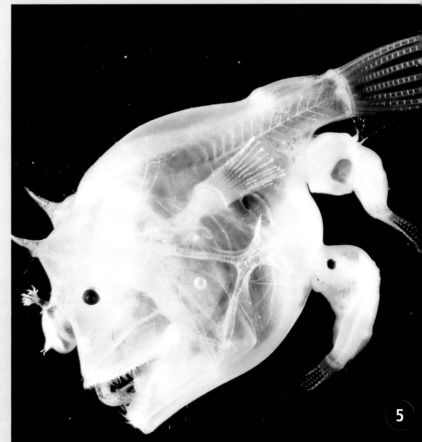

Salt Water and Fresh Water

Oceans are full of salt water. In fact, ocean water contains about 4 ounces (118 mL) of salt per gallon (4 L) of water. Ocean salts contain sodium, similar to table salt, and many other elements as well.

The salt in ocean water comes from **minerals**. Minerals are found in soil and rocks. Water carries soil and rocks into rivers and lakes. The water in rivers and lakes flows into the oceans.

Over time, ocean water **evaporates**, but the salt does not. This very slowly raises the levels of salt in the ocean. About 3 to 3.5 percent of ocean water is salt.

▓ Freshwater lakes make up almost 88 percent of the world's fresh surface water.

Fresh water has very little salt. Most lakes and rivers are fresh water. Still, some lakes have salt water.

About half the water a person uses each day comes from freshwater lakes and rivers. The rest of the water comes from **groundwater**. Fresh water weighs less than salt water because it has fewer minerals. It is easier to float in salt water than fresh water.

EARTH'S WATER SUPPLY

This illustration shows how Earth's water supply is broken down in terms of fresh and salt water, as well as ice.

97%
Salt Water

2.25%
Permanent Ice

0.75%
Fresh Water

Oceans

The world's oceans are one big body of water known as the world ocean. The **continents** divide this body of water into the five oceans. The ocean floor has mountains, volcanoes, and valleys.

More than one million species of plants and animals are known to live in the ocean. Ocean creatures can be tiny like shrimp or large like whales.

The world's largest mammal is the blue whale. It grows to between 80 and 110 feet (24 and 34 meters) in length and weighs up to 240,000 pounds (108,862 kilograms). Plankton are the smallest creatures in the ocean. They are tiny floating plants and animals. Many fish and whales feed on plankton.

From space, Earth appears mostly blue in color. Some scientists think Earth should have been named Oceanus.

Oceans are also home to many types of plants, including algae, kelp, and seaweed. These plants provide food and habitats for ocean life.

People have been exploring the ocean for centuries. Sailing ships, submarines, and underwater breathing gear have been used to help people learn more about the ocean's plants and animals.

OCEAN ZONES

The ocean has five main zones, or depth levels. Each zone is based on the level of sunlight an area receives.

The epipelagic, or sunlight, zone is the ocean's shallow, top layer. This layer extends about 656 feet (200 m) below the water's surface. Here, there is enough sunlight for plants to survive.

The mesopelagic, or twilight, zone is located 656 to 3,281 feet (200 to 1,000 m) below the ocean's surface. This zone receives very little sunlight. Plants cannot live in this region.

The bathypalagic, or midnight, zone is located about 3,281 to 13,123 feet (1,000 to 4,000 m) below the water's surface. Sunlight does not reach this deep ocean area.

The abyssal zone is located 13,123 to 19,685 feet (4,000 to 6,000 m) below the ocean's surface. This zone is dark. The water in this region is near freezing temperature.

The hadal zone is located 19,685 to 36,089 feet (6,000 to 11,000 m) below the ocean's surface. The ocean's deepest **trenches** are found in the hadal zone.

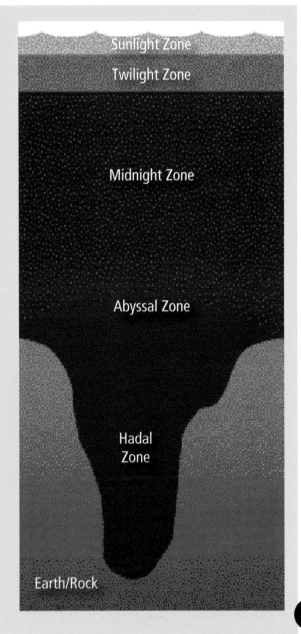

Sunlight Zone

Twilight Zone

Midnight Zone

Abyssal Zone

Hadal Zone

Earth/Rock

Oceans, Lakes, and Rivers Around the World

ARCTIC OCEAN

Mackenzie River
Great Bear Lake
Great Slave Lake
Lake Winnipeg
NORTH AMERICA
Lake Tahoe
Missouri River
Rio Grande
Mississippi River
Lake Huron

Lake Superior
Lake Superior is the largest freshwater lake on Earth. It covers more than 51,000 miles (82,000 km) of land. Lake Superior holds enough water to fill all of the other Great Lakes and still have enough water left to fill Lake Erie three times.

ATLANTIC OCEAN

Lake Maracaibo

PACIFIC OCEAN

SOUTH AMERICA

Amazon River
South America's Amazon River is the largest river in the world in terms of water flow. The river collects water from the Amazon Rain Forest, which is the largest and wettest rain forest in the world.

Lake Titicaca
Lake Titicaca in Peru is the highest lake in the world that can be navigated by boat. It is about 12,500 feet (3,810 m) above **sea level**. Lake Titicaca is also the second largest freshwater lake in South America.

N
W E
S
621 Miles
0   1,000 Kilometers

WHAT HAVE YOU LEARNED ABOUT OCEANS, LAKES, AND RIVERS?

This map shows the location of oceans, as well as major lakes and rivers around the world. Use this map, and research online to answer these questions.

1. Find the place where you live on the map. Does the place where you live border an ocean? If not, which ocean is nearest to your home? Which countries border each ocean?
2. Which major rivers and lakes are closest to the place where you live?

ASIA

Ladoga Lake

EUROPE

Lake Balkhash

Lake Baikal
Siberia, Russia, is home to the world's deepest lake. Lake Baikal is 5,369 feet (1,638 m) deep. That is more than 1 mile (1.6 km) straight down.

Rhine River

Volga River

Danube River

Indus River

Euphrates River

Tigris River

Niger River

Ganges River

Yangtze River

PACIFIC OCEAN

AFRICA

Lake Tanganyika

Congo River

Lake Victoria

Lake Malawi

ATLANTIC OCEAN

INDIAN OCEAN

AUSTRALIA

Murray-Darling River

Nile River
The Nile River in Egypt is the longest river in the world. It is 4,132 miles (6,650 km) long. The Nile flows through nine countries and empties into the Mediterranean Sea.

Mariana Trench
Mariana Trench in the Pacific Ocean is the deepest spot in any ocean. It is about 35,797 feet (10,911 m) deep. This is deep enough to completely sink the tallest mountain in the world, Mount Everest, which is 29,035 feet (8,850 m) tall.

SOUTHERN OCEAN

ANTARCTICA

Lakes and Rivers

Lakes form when water settles in a **depression**, or a low spot in the ground. Lakes can form anywhere in the world. Over time, they can disappear. When water in a lake evaporates, it disappears. Some lakes are called seas. Usually, this means the lake contains salt water.

The largest lakes in the world are the Caspian Sea, between Europe and Asia, Lake Victoria, in Africa, and Lake Superior, partly in Ontario, Canada, and partly in the state of Michigan.

A river is a body of flowing water. **Gravity** causes rivers to flow from high to low ground. Rivers flow into lakes and other rivers, which flow into oceans.

Most cities and towns are built near rivers. Rivers are used to water crops, ship goods, and to provide water for drinking. Rivers can also be used to make electricity. The United States has more than 250,000 rivers, totaling about 3.5 million miles (5.6 million km) in length. Humans depend on rivers for survival.

Red Sea bannerfish live mainly near the coral reef areas of several seas in the Middle East.

Some types of fish or animals can only live in salt water or oceans. Others can only live in freshwater lakes and rivers. A few kinds of animals, such as the bull shark, can live in both salt water and fresh water.

Freshwater fish or animals can be small or large. The smallest creatures in rivers and lakes include clams, snails, and worms. Larger animals include many fish species, such as rainbow trout and salmon.

THE EFFECT OF PRECIPITATION

Precipitation plays a key role in the creation and maintenance of a freshwater **biome**. Water falls to Earth as precipitation. When the water falls, some seeps into the soil to form groundwater. The soil absorbs some, but not all, of the water. The remaining rain becomes runoff and runs over the surface of the land. Over time, it becomes rivers, streams, lakes, and ponds. These fresh waters form networks that connect to one another.

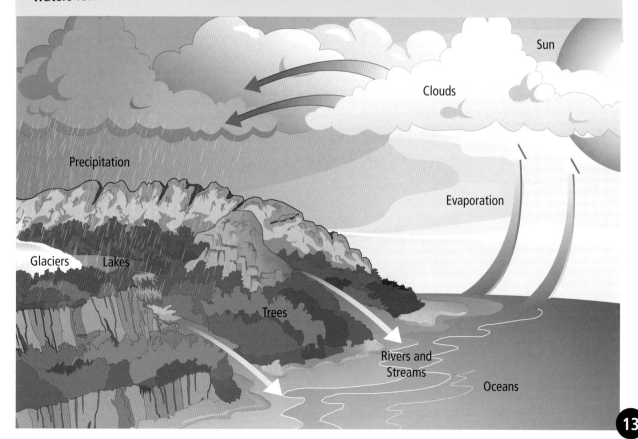

Sun

Clouds

Precipitation

Evaporation

Glaciers   Lakes

Trees

Rivers and Streams

Oceans

Living Underwater

Almost every stretch of open water on Earth is home to some kind of life. In fact, 80 percent of life on Earth is found under the ocean's surface.

PLANKTON

- Plankton are floating or drifting plants and animals. They cannot be seen by the naked eye.
- Plankton plants are called phytoplankton.
- Phytoplanktons are most numerous near shores where there is more sunlight.
- Plankton animals are called zooplankton. Zooplankton include copepods, jellyfish, and arrow worms.

NEKTON

- Most underwater animals are nekton.
- Nekton can swim without the help of flowing **currents**.
- They often live in areas where there is a certain temperature, food supply, and salt solution in the water.
- Examples of nekton include sharks, eels, octopuses, sea turtles, and other fish.

BENTHOS

- Benthos are animals and plants that live on the bottom of the ocean.
- Some benthos animals, such as oysters, remain in one place their entire lives.
- Others, such as starfish and lobsters, move by swimming or walking.
- Benthos plants can only grow in areas of the ocean that sunlight reaches.
- All benthos plants are attached to the ocean floor.

Underwater life ranges in size from the largest animal on Earth to creatures too small to be seen with the naked eye. All of these plant and animal species have adapted to living in or near fresh waters.

INSECTS

- Some insects live their whole lives in the water. Others live there for only part of their lives.
- The **larvae** of many insects, such as mosquitoes and dragonflies, live in fresh water. They leave the water at adulthood.

REPTILES AND AMPHIBIANS

- Reptiles, such as snakes and lizards, as well as amphibians, such as frogs and salamanders, live in fresh water.
- Amphibians live part of their lives in water. As larvae, they often eat aquatic plants. As adults, they mainly eat insects.

BIRDS AND MAMMALS

- Many species of wading birds, waterfowl, and shorebirds live in freshwater biomes.
- Some species use riverbanks or the shores of lakes or ponds as places to nest.
- Mammals that spend part of their time in the water include beavers and muskrats.

FISH

- There are two types of freshwater fish.
- The first type are **parasites**. They attach to other animals and suck their blood.
- The second type are bony fishes, such as salmon or trout. They eat plant food or other aquatic animals.

PLANTS

- Aquatic plants are grouped by where they grow in the water.
- Submergent plants grow under the water. Even the leaves are below the surface.
- Floating aquatic plants float on the water's surface.

Water Uses

People use water to drink, wash, clean, and cook. Only about one percent of the world's water can be easily used by people. Humans can have large effects on the sources of water they use. The Aral Sea is a large lake in the Middle East. Using water for farming has caused the lake to shrink 60 percent over the past 30 years.

Water can also carry pollution from human activity. In the Mississippi River, there is a large area called a dead zone. It is near the river's mouth in the Gulf of Mexico. The dead zone covers thousands of square miles (km) and contains so much pollution that no plant or animal can live there.

It is important to protect oceans, lakes, and rivers so that people can continue to enjoy them. Polluted oceans, lakes, and rivers cannot be used for swimming or fishing.

■ About 4.5 million gallons of water flow through the Mississippi River at New Orleans every second. That is equal to about 166 semitrailers full of water moving through the city each second.

Water Pollution Timeline

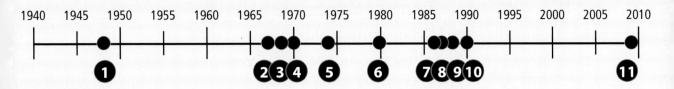

1940 1945 1950 1955 1960 1965 1970 1975 1980 1985 1990 1995 2000 2005 2010

1 **2 3 4** **5** **6** **7 8 9 10** **11**

1 **1948**
Congress passes the Water Pollution Control Act. This is Congress's first major act dealing with water pollution.

2 **1967**
The *Torrey Canyon* oil tanker spills more than 29 million gallons (109 million liters) of oil off the coast of England.

3 **1969**
Ohio's Cuyahoga River bursts into flames from oil and chemical pollution. Flames shoot high into the air, causing more than $50,000 in damage.

4 **1970**
President Nixon creates the Environmental Protection Agency (EPA).

5 **1974**
The Safe Drinking Water Act is passed by Congress. This federal law ensures that people in the United States have access to safe drinking water.

6 **1980**
Several hundred families in the Love Canal area of Niagara Falls, New York, are forced to move due to toxic waste placed in the area by a chemical company.

7 **1987–1988**
Medical waste, including syringes, washes up along beaches of the Jersey Shore communities in New Jersey.

8 **1988**
Congress passes the Ocean Dumping Ban Act. The act makes dumping municipal, industrial, and medical waste into the ocean illegal.

9 **1989**
An oil tanker named *Exxon Valdez* spills about 11 million gallons (41.64 million liters) of crude oil into the sea. The spill results in a 3,000-square-mile (4,828-square-kilometer) oil slick and kills hundreds of thousands of animals.

10 **1990**
The 20th anniversary of Earth Day is celebrated by 140 countries.

11 **2009**
The United States Supreme Court rules that cost-benefit analysis can be used in environmental cases. In such cases, the cost of protecting the environment is weighed against the cost of damage caused if no action is taken to help the environment.

Protecting Water

Oceans, lakes, and rivers are not only sources of water. They are habitats for life forms. Many types of plants and animals make their home in water. Oceans, lakes, and rivers also hold resources such as oil, minerals, and food.

The United States has many laws to protect oceans, lakes, and rivers. The laws protect the plants and animals that live in these bodies of water. There are also rules to keep the water safe to drink. In 1972, Congress created clean water laws. As a result, some water surfaces today are cleaner. However, water pollution remains a serious problem in the United States and around the world.

■ Just one quart (1 L) of motor oil can cause an oil slick almost 10,000 square yards (8,000 square meters) in size. Oil can cause severe harm to plants and animals that depend on water.

Plastic waste from shipping and seaside communities has been collecting in the ocean for many years. Currents have brought together an island of floating plastic trash between Hawai'i and the west coast of North America. This patch of floating garbage is twice the size of Texas. Many birds and fish have died from eating the plastic waste. Fish that eat plastic absorb toxic chemicals in their body. These fish are harmful if eaten by people. To help keep plastic waste out of the water, people can use fewer disposable products and **recycle** often.

What is an Oceanographer?

Oceanographers study the ocean floor, currents, water, and **tides**. Scientists can learn a great deal from the oceans. New medicines and foods have been discovered by studying oceans.

Studying water helps scientists predict long-term weather. Scientists can also learn how people and animals change water.

Jacques Cousteau

Jacques Cousteau, a French naval officer, was well known for underwater exploration. He invented the self-contained underwater breathing apparatus, or S.C.U.B.A. This is a tank that allows divers to breathe underwater.

Cousteau was also known for the movies he made while exploring underwater. Two of his movies, *The Silent World* and *World Without Sun*, won Academy Awards. Cousteau also had his own television show called T*he Undersea World of Jacques Cousteau*. On this show, Cousteau talked about what he found during his underwater explorations.

WORKING CONDITIONS
Oceanographers must spend a large amount of their time doing research in or on water.

SAFETY
Waves, high tides, and some underwater animals can pose a danger to oceanographers.

Regulator

EQUIPMENT
Oceanographers use computer models and satellite information to learn more about the ocean. When working in the water, they must wear special diving gear. For example, regulators help divers breathe underwater.

Eight Facts About Oceans, Lakes, and Rivers

Lake Tahoe, on the border of California and Nevada, contains enough water for every U.S. citizen to use 50 gallons (189 L) per day for five years.

The Nile River in Egypt is one of the largest rivers on Earth. It drains water from an area of 1,293,000 square miles (3,349,000 sq. km).

Nearly half of the world's lakes are located in Canada.

The world's largest ocean is the Pacific Ocean. It covers about one-third of Earth.

Oceans cover about 140 million square miles (361 million sq. km) of Earth's surface.

The average depth of the ocean is more than 2.5 miles (4 km).

Ocean ridges form a great mountain range through all of Earth's oceans. The range is nearly 40,000 miles (64,000 km) long.

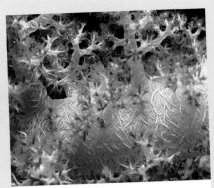

A mouthful of ocean water can contain hundreds of thousands of plankton.

Oceans, Lakes, and Rivers Brain Teasers

1 What name do some scientists think Earth should have been given?

2 Which ocean is the largest?

3 How much of Earth is covered by water?

4 How much of the world's water is salt water?

5 Do objects float better in salt water or fresh water?

6 What is the world's largest animal?

7 What is a scientist who studies oceans called?

8 Who was Jacques Cousteau?

9 What are the names of the five oceans?

10 Name the longest river in the world.

Science in Action

See the Difference

This experiment will show the differences between salt water and fresh water.

Tools Needed

1 fresh egg

1 large glass

water

salt

spoon

Directions

1 Fill the glass with fresh water. Carefully, add the egg to the glass of fresh water. Watch what happens.

2 Remove the egg from the glass of fresh water. Next, stir some salt into the glass of water. Carefully, place the egg in the water. Watch what happens.

3 Did the egg float better in salt water or fresh water? Why?

Words to Know

biome: a major region of land that is defined by the plants and animals that live there

continents: the seven large land masses on Earth; Africa, Antarctica, Asia, Australia, Europe, North America, and South America

currents: paths along which a body of water moves

depression: a low spot in the ground

ecosystems: communities of plants and animals and the physical environment in which they live

evaporates: changes from a liquid or solid to a gas

gravity: the force that pulls objects toward the center of Earth

groundwater: water beneath Earth's surface

habitats: the natural places where plants and animals live

larvae: the young, wormlike form of many insects

minerals: natural substances that are not an animal or plant

parasites: organisms that depend on other organisms to survive

pollution: when water or air is made dirty by harmful materials such as gases, chemicals, and waste

recycle: return a material to its original condition so a process can begin again

sea level: the level of the ocean's surface

tides: the regular rise and fall of water level in the oceans, caused by the pull of the Sun and Moon on Earth

Index

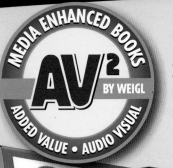

Log on to www.av2books.com

AV² by Weigl brings you media enhanced books that support active learning. Go to **www.av2books.com**, and enter the special code inside the front cover of this book. You will gain access to enriched and enhanced content that supplements and complements this book. Content includes video, audio, web links, quizzes, a slide show, and activities.

Audio
Listen to sections of the book read aloud.

Video
Watch informative video clips.

Web Link
Find research sites and play interactive games.

Try This!
Complete activities and hands-on experiments.

WHAT'S ONLINE?

Try This!
Complete activities and hands-on experiments.

Web Link
Find research sites and play interactive games.

Video
Watch informative video clips.

EXTRA FEATURES

Pages 8-9 Try this activity about the ocean zones

Pages 10-11 See if you can identify oceans, lakes, and rivers around the world

Pages 16-17 Use this timeline activity to test your knowledge of world events

Pages 18-19 Write about a day in the life of an oceanographer

Page 22 Try the activity in the book, then play an interactive game

Pages 6-7 Link to more information about fresh and salt water

Pages 12-13 Find out more about lakes, rivers, and the water cycle

Pages 18-19 Learn more about being an oceanographer

Page 20 Link to facts about oceans, lakes, and rivers

Pages 4-5 Watch a video about oceans, lakes, and rivers

Pages 8-9 Check out a video about oceans

Pages 14-15 View underwater life in its natural surroundings

Audio
Hear introductory audio at the top of every page.

Key Words
Study vocabulary, and play a matching word game.

Slide Show
View images and captions, and try a writing activity.

AV² Quiz
Take this quiz to test your knowledge

Due to the dynamic nature of the Internet, some of the URLs and activities provided as part of AV² by Weigl may have changed or ceased to exist. AV² by Weigl accepts no responsibility for any such changes. All media enhanced books are regularly monitored to update addresses and sites in a timely manner. Contact AV² by Weigl at 1-866-649-3445 or av2books@weigl.com with any questions, comments, or feedback.